28 WAYS
TO MAKE IT A CHOICE
TO HAVE GREAT STYLE
(ON ANY BUDGET)

28 WAYS
TO MAKE IT A CHOICE TO HAVE GREAT STYLE (ON ANY BUDGET)

WRITTEN BY
KANIKA STARR REYNOLDS

Copyright © 2022 by Kanika Starr Reynolds

VMH Publishing
Atlanta, GA
www.vmhpublishing.net

Without limiting the rights under copyright reserved above, no part of this publication may be reproduced, stored in or introduced into a retrieval system, or transmitted, in any form or any means.

Manufactured in the United States of America

Paperback ISBN: 978-1-0879-4917-8

EBook: 978-1-0879-4925-3

10 9 8 7 6 5 4 3 2 1

Publisher's Note:

The publisher is not responsible for the content of this book nor websites, or social media pages (or their content) that are not owned by the publisher.

DEDICATION

THIS BOOK IS DEDICATED TO my friend, Kari Cartwright. Thank you for always seeing me as fabulous (fabulous was your favorite word). I remember you asking me to consult with you about your image ten years ago. You even had a dream that we were shopping together! That was never a reality, but a seed was planted. I wrote a book to help many women get the desired results to be fabulous. We never got to shop together, but I know you're fabulous in heaven. Rest in peace, fabulously!

Rest in peace, Max Azria. You are indeed the designer I've loved the longest. The designer that made me feel like you knew me and what I would wear. Thank you for the vision behind BCBG, my absolute favorite fashion brand. BCBG stood for Bon Chic, Bon Genre, interpreted to mean "good style, good attitude." I found out its meaning the day I heard of your passing. I knew it was a reason I felt so good wearing my BCBG pieces, because good style can definitely give you a good attitude.

Mom, even at seventy-one, the age you are at the time this book was printed, you're still fabulous. Thanks for passing that down to my sister, April, and me.

THE HEART OF WHY I WROTE THIS BOOK

FINALLY, I DEDICATE THIS BOOK to women who give so much to their family that they have forgotten to take time out for themselves. My personal testimony is that I loved fashion from a young age. I got married young and after marriage, I needed to rediscover who I was and the image I would create as a wife. I didn't want to disrespect my husband in appearance or conduct. After we had children, there was another responsibility for me to be appropriate as a mother and make my children proud because I didn't want to embarrass them either. I was very modest, making sure my clothes covered my arms and legs and anything else that would draw too much attention to my body parts that are sacred. My shapely legs are one of the best features of my body and I covered them with long skirts. I was like a fish out of the water, not knowing what my image should be as a wife or as a mother. Over time, I've discovered, as a mother, that it's for the benefit of our children that we don't totally lose who we are after having them. Beauty is confidence in your uniqueness and that's something that only you can contribute to the world. It's also important to remember why our spouse married us. Keep yourself up. Just because we're married doesn't mean we get a pass to be frumpy. If you've lost a piece of yourself, get your confidence back! I pray that this book taps into the diva in you. I pray that it builds your confidence and you're filled with the possibilities of regaining whatever you lost. It's not selfish to take care of yourself; it is self-care. May your inner and outer beauty give other people confidence to live their true beauty as well. The world is indeed a stage and you are the star, so don't try and hide your shine!

CONTENTS

Chapter 1 : Having Great Style Is About Having Great Confidence 1

Chapter 2: What's In Your Closet? 10

Chapter 3: Foundation Is Fundamental The Importance Of Undergarments 15

Chapter 4: Pretty Takes Preparation 17

Chapter 5: Find A Style Muse 22

Chapter 6: Personalize Your Style Personal 25

Chapter 7: Be A Diva On A Dime (Vintage, Flea Market, Thrift) 28

Chapter 8: Become A Great Shopper 32

Chapter 9: Jeans 37

Chapter 10: The Black Dress 41

Chapter 11: Sunday Best................................... 45

Chapter 12: Date Night Dressing...................... 47

Chapter 13: The Style Success For The Working Diva 49

Chapter 14: Sleep Pretty 54

Chapter 15: Travel Fabulous.............................. 57

Chapter 16: Purses, Hand Bags, And
　　　　　　Other Bags 63
Chapter 17: Shoes 68
Chapter 18: Basic Etiquette 72
Chapter 19: Dress For Your Age 77
Chapter 20: Worthy Workout Wear 81
Chapter 21: Accessorize, Accessorize,
　　　　　　Accessorize 83
Chapter 22: Skirts 90
Chapter 23: Outerwear For The Outdoors 92
Chapter 24: When To Splurge And When
　　　　　　To Save 96
Chapter 25: Perfume 103
Chapter 26: Picture Perfect 107
Chapter 27: Self-Love And Self-Care 110
Chapter 28: Have Finesse 115

PROLOGUE

SINCE THE DAYS OF MY youth, I've loved to get dressed up. Growing up, my mom worked at a department store and made sure I was neat and groomed. I had no say in the matter. I knew I was a neat and groomed child because the hit television sitcom the *Cosby Show* was being watched in just about every home, and the character Rudy Huxtable on the show would wear the exact same sweaters as me. When I saw that what was on television was in my closet, it made me feel like a celebrity and heightened my love of fashion all the more. Although my love for fashion started young, I really honed my style as a teenager while reading teen fashion magazines. Those magazines gave me inspiration and I was determined to express myself. I added my own style to the afflatus that I had carefully gleaned from turning page after page. I would tear out the pages of the fashion magazine and shop for similar looks. By the time I was in high school, I had my own style, which consisted of vintage, eclectic, and prim.

I woke up each morning excited to get dressed and show my creative look. The confidence I felt about my image was the beginning of me making it a choice to have a great day because I was making it a choice to have great style! I didn't know then that fashion would be such a big part of me, but to some degree it's the essence of my total being. I took time with my appearance. My love for fashion started so young that it's pure. It also taught me the valuable lesson, that people treat you how they perceive you. We play a role in how we're perceived, so dress in a respectful manner so that you get respect.

At a young age we heard that we should focus on a person's inside and not on the outward appearance, and although that is true, we live in a world that judges the outside first. Why is this? Because it's the first thing we see! This is why no matter how we feel, we should get up, get dressed, and look our best so we feel our best! We must let the world know that we love ourselves and that love will teach other people how to love us in return, and if the world doesn't love us, at least by our appearance they will respect us. When we hold ourselves to a high standard, nobody has the power to lower that standard. We hold the power.

We are made in the image of God (Genesis 1:27) and in the words of one of my favorite pastors "If God is our Father; we should look like Him!" Our Heavenly Father is a King and we are His heirs representing royalty. Put on your imaginary tiara (or real one if you have it). Turn the page, Queen, it's time to dress like the royalty that you are!

CHAPTER 1

HAVING GREAT STYLE IS ABOUT HAVING GREAT CONFIDENCE

Nothing makes a woman more beautiful than the belief that she is beautiful. – Sophia Loren

THERE IS NO STYLE WITHOUT confidence. Women of great style know who they are and knowing who you are exudes confidence. A confident woman doesn't have to follow the trends because she can create them. The more you know yourself the better your style will be defined, and knowing yourself does not happen overnight. You learn yourself by paying attention to the things that you like and things that you dislike. You also learn yourself by starting good small habits done daily and being intentional about them. Don't be discouraged by the process; it takes some time. When we're young, we start out excited about who and what we can become, and then before we know it, we start to settle without much thought about who and what our circumstances have made us. Unexpected things happen, marriage happens, children happen, life happens. If we don't make time to make ourselves a priority, we unknowingly end up existing instead of being, creating, and living our most fabulous confident life. We have to create and cultivate the woman we want to become because it does not happen on its own. It's crucial for us to take the time to get to know who we are because in turn we know who we are not. Confidence will affect every area of our life, but my goal is to help you become confident with great style. Let's be clear; it may not be fair but we are judged by our appearance and we are responsible for the image that other people see. People will treat us how they perceive us. From this day on, I want you to be mindful of that—you can be treated differently by how you present yourself. The goal is to look your best everywhere you go so that you are treated in the direct proportion (if not better) than how you carry yourself. What is needed is a confidence that can only come from inside. Take time to put yourself together. This small sacrifice of waking up early to get yourself together properly brings big rewards. Be the best that you can be.

A well-groomed man or woman makes a statement to the world that they care about themselves and the respect they have for themselves is what they expect from others. That is why I want you to pay close attention to the things you wear that make you feel good, the colors that compliment your skin tone, the garments that accentuate your best features, and the things that get you noticed. Style confidence is about self-confidence; feeling fabulous on the outside starts with feeling fabulous on the inside. I know that for some people reading this, you may not feel fabulous, so it's hard to look fabulous, but let me encourage you that when you feel your worst is when you look your best! Don't dress like how you feel; dress like how you want to feel!

Tips on Building Confidence

Loving the skin you're in starts with not comparing yourself to other people. We live in a world inundated with outside input. Social media and celebrities show all of the airbrush, highlights, and edits, so be careful not to feel bad about you while watching them. It's interesting how one childhood tease or thing that you don't like about yourself can be a focal point of insecurity for much of your life! Many times it builds a complex and inside you don't feel beautiful, so the outside reflects how you feel on the inside. It's important to never get your mind stuck on what you cannot change. Focus on what can be improved. Some of the things that we tend to not like we cover up, and those are the things that make us unique and are meant to stand out. I had long sideburns when I was a teenager and my brother would tease me. I'd cut them off and they would grow right back. Then the singer Toni Braxton hit the mainstream and came out with a video rocking a short haircut with long sideburns, and all of a sudden, my sideburns were popular! The sideburns that were once talked about became my trademark.

There are some things that we may not like that can't be changed, so we have to change how we look at it. There are other things that we will like about ourselves and those are the things that we play up. Highlight everything that you love about you. Be happy with who you are and embrace your uniqueness. You are fearfully and wonderfully made and there's nobody else in the world like you! I read a quote recently that explains why self-esteem and self-love are so important. It read: "Love yourself so you don't lose yourself in people who don't love you." – unknown

Exercises to do to improve self-esteem:

Highlight what you love about yourself. (You may have to ask close family and friends about your highlights and that's fine; they may see what you've overlooked. It's also fine if it's difficult to find all ten of your highlights and it's also fine if you have more. It's all about discovering your fabulousness that is sitting dormant. The better you know yourself the easier this becomes.)

Highlight 1

Highlight 2

Highlight 3

Highlight 4

Highlight 5

Highlight 6

Highlight 7

Highlight 8

Highlight 9

Highlight 10

Find pictures of yourself when you felt confident and looked your best. It's a reminder that the "it" girl is still there; she just needs to be rediscovered.

Pictures

Pictures

*A Thought to Remember:

Set some goals of the things that you need to work on. Do you need to smile more, start exercising, are you shy and need practice striking up a conversation with a stranger to practice confidence in that area? Whatever it is, this is your space to jot it down and start working on it. Remember, small goals done daily lead to big results over time.

Goal 1

Goal 2

Goal 3

Goal 4

Goal 5

If loving yourself is hard to do, then keep being intentional about it until it's as natural as water rolling off of a duck's back! It will be such a game changer for your life. There is no one else in all of the world like you and the world is in great need of your confidence in knowing that! You are uniquely made for such a time as this. A healthy self-confidence is the beginning of great style!

CHAPTER 2

WHAT'S IN YOUR CLOSET?

YOUR CLOSET NEEDS TO BE a place of joy and celebration of who you are now, not who you were. – Stacey London

We can tell a lot about people by many things. The books they read, the people they are around, and how they dress! We can even tell a person's mood by the clothes they wear. Have you ever worn dark colors when you feel down? What about when you're in good spirits? Do you wear bold and vibrant colors? Just like moods affect our choices in what to wear, your closet also reflects your personality and how you feel about yourself. If I toured your closet, I could tell if you're organized or chaotic, conservative or liberal; the closet will tell it, the closet won't lie. It's no question the closet speaks volumes about a person. The question is, what is your closet saying? There's a chance that you would like your style to speak a new language or else you wouldn't be reading this book. Before we get into the meat and potatoes of style, it's time to see what you're already working with. What should stay or what needs to be eliminated in your closet. After confidence comes the importance of the closet. Remember, your closet, reflects you.

1. Cleanse your closet – There are some clothes that are in your closet that are too small, too large, out of style, and some that are just taking up space. First thing's first; get a full-length mirror and schedule some time to try on clothes. All of them. Especially the clothes that you haven't worn in the last year. Start with the clothes that are in season at the moment. If it's summer, try on summer clothes, and if it's winter, try on winter clothes. This may be a project that takes time, so prioritize the importance by breaking it down by the season you're in. Then ask yourself this question: "Do I love this dress?" or "do I love this shirt?" If you love it, then start a keep-it pile—as long as it's worthy of being kept! Then ask yourself these questions: "Does it fit well and does

it flatter me? If it doesn't fit well and it cost too much to be tailored, it can be sold to a consignment shop and you can use the money to buy new clothes that fit and flatter. Maybe there is someone you want to bless that can fit those too-big or too-small clothes; then be a blessing and you will be blessed. The key is to purge your closet from anything that doesn't line up with the stylish woman you desire to become. You may have heard the saying: "Dress for the job you want." I agree. I also will add, "Look great while doing the job you have." Pay attention to dominant colors and prints that speak to you. What colors make you feel bold and powerful? Are you partial to stripes or polka dots? Do you have a lot of black in your closet? Maybe it's time for some color! Our closet leaves clues of our style and you want your closet to say, "I have style, great style!"

2. Organize – Now that you've gotten rid of the unwanted, unused, and outdated attire, organize what's left. Everything has a place. Skirts belong with other skirts, sundresses should all hang together. It's even a good

idea to color code. It makes getting dressed easier. The clothes that made the cut to stay in your closet are the choices that you can mix and match, and they make you feel the most fabulous. This is the foundation to great style, walking into your closet and looking at the pieces that express who you are and feeling proud of the selections that you chose to represent your image.

3. There are treasures right there in your closet – There are some articles of clothing that you may have forgotten about that were hidden behind things that no longer fit who you're becoming. Pull those fabulous finds to the front of the closet as reminders to wear them.

4. Get a corkboard and hang pictures of fashion inspiration from magazines to give ideas on how to chicly put together what's in your closet. You can take several pictures for different occasions and get them developed into a picture, then hang it on your board. This way you will always be ready, even if it's last minute; just refer to your inspiration board.

5. Keep some interesting prints in your closet because they make great conversation pieces.

6. Now that you've purged and only have the things that make you feel your best, shop your closet! One of the best things that's ever happened to me is filing bankruptcy. Before then, I spent a lot of money at the mall and department stores using credit cards and spending money that I didn't have. Shopping was my addiction! The bankruptcy changed all of that because I no longer had credit cards to use. However, the loss became the win. I was faced with the reality that I couldn't shop like I used to, but I had enough clothes in my closet to shop my own closet! I developed prowess in mixing and matching what I already had. The creativity galvanized a love for using what I had and making it look good without the need to spend money. Everything I needed, I already had!

CHAPTER 3

FOUNDATION IS FUNDAMENTAL

The Importance of Undergarments

Impeccable style starts with the foundation of good undergarments. – Kanika Starr Reynolds

JUST LIKE THE FOUNDATION OF a house is the most important component of the house, the foundation of our wardrobe is our undergarments. Not just bra and panties but girdles and Spanx, if they are needed, to nip, tuck, and hide so that we appear more slender. A girdle will smooth out the wrinkles and make clothes look better creating a slimmer waistline. Unfortunately, many women put the main focus on the outer apparel, not realizing undergarments—which people don't see—make what can be seen look better. Make it a priority to invest in good undergarments, panties, bras, and foundational pieces such as Spanx. Undergarments are well worth the investment, and when they are pretty, it makes you feel good while getting dressed. It will feel good to be able to take off your clothes and like the panties and bra that only you can see. Remember, undergarments are just that—they go underneath garments, and even if they are pretty, it's not for all to see. Classy women know that some things should be discreet and what's underneath our clothes is one of them. So keep them pretty, clean, and in good shape. The world may not see it, but you'll know you're fabulous, all of you, both seen and unseen.

Here are a few bras that you should be in your wardrobe:
- Strapless bra
- Convertible bra
- T-Shirt bra

The bra you wear should be based on the size of your breasts. Women with larger breasts will need a full-cup bra and women with smaller breasts will appreciate the push-up bra. The most important thing is getting measured every six months by a bra-fitting specialist to make sure your bra fits well and to discuss what bra is right for you. Good undergarments will help the overall look appear neat and polished.

CHAPTER 4

PRETTY TAKES PREPARATION

There are no ugly women, only lazy ones.
– Helena Rubinstein

NO MATTER HOW RUN-OF-THE-MILL THE event, party, or even company picnic is, put thought into looking your best while attending it! The truth of the matter is that it is better to be overdressed than underdressed. It doesn't have to be a red-carpet reception for you to look red-carpet ready. This doesn't have to be stressful, because stress is never beautiful. How you eliminate the stress of finding the appropriate apparel for an event or occasion is by preparing in advance. Here are some things to remember while preparing to dress to impress and look your best. I have a motto that I try to live by: stay ready so you don't have to get ready! Here's a checklist of some important questions you need to answer and things you should do to keep you prepared for any occasion.

What kind of event will you be attending? Is this an event for work? If it's a wedding, is it an outdoor wedding or indoor wedding? A baby shower or first date? Check to see if there is a dress code or a theme on the invitation. If you're invited to a restaurant, check their dress code online because upper-echelon restaurants will specify one. Always check in advance to see what you already have before you buy something new! It may be a dress you've already worn but a new belt or jewelry can give it a whole new look! If the dress doesn't fit, the shoes are uncomfortable, or the clutch is missing rhinestones, then this is the time to write down only what you need for this event and shop a few stores so you can look for sales and clearance items. Giving yourself time gives you options; you don't have to settle for the first thing you see. You can get the best quality you can afford in your price range. (CHAPTER 7 will give you tips on how to make the most of your shopping experience.)

Once you've done inventory of what you already have or shopped for a few missing links, then take a full-length picture in the mirror from head to toe, front and back so that you will see what everyone else will see. Two things that will not lie is the mirror and the camera! Edit and make changes accordingly. You may need longer earrings or different shoes but let the long-length mirror and the picture tell you. Keep trying on and switching out until everything is to your liking. It may seem like an inconvenience at the beginning to shop and try on different clothes days or weeks in advance, but when the day for you to shine arrives, it will be well worth it to feel confident in that moment. Your preparation will make you feel like the most beautiful girl in the room, but don't forget your smile and confidence; they are the most beautiful accessories you will have!

Other important details that will help you shine brightly:

Whiten teeth with Crest White Strips or other brand of teeth whiteners that can be purchased at a retailer, no dentist necessary.

Schedule your hair appointment in advance. Get any major hair changes like color or cuts weeks before to adjust to your new look or to see what changes may have to be made if you don't like it.

Get your manicure close to the time of the event to make sure there is no chipped nail polish. If you're wearing open-toe shoes, make sure your pedicure is also done.

Schedule your underarm wax or shave underarm hair yourself. Wear a clear deodorant to prevent stains on clothes and avoid clumping deodorant under your armpits.

Do an undergarment check, make sure waist trainers, bra straps, and panty lines are not visible. Your dress should look smooth without lines showing.

Walk in shoes beforehand to make sure that the heel isn't too tall and that they're sturdy. You should always look graceful while walking. If your legs wobble excessively while walking in your high-heel shoes, those aren't the shoes to wear.

Check the weather to make sure you don't need a shawl, scarf, or outerwear. Make sure to take a cute umbrella if it rains.

Make sure your clutch/handbag has all of your necessities in it before a big event. Is it big enough to carry your cell phone and keys? For evening events and weddings, smaller bags look more polished; leave your big work bag at home.

Walk straight and poised.

Remember to spray on just a touch of perfume; too much perfume can overwhelm. Just enough perfume completes an outfit.

CHAPTER 5

FIND A STYLE MUSE

When the student is ready the teacher will appear.
– Unknown

IT'S HARD TO GET WHERE we are trying to go without learning from someone already there. That's why a style mentor is so important. We follow people on social media for recipes, politics, and entertainment. Find someone to follow who has great style. Another way to glean great style is to observe keenly the fabulous fashion all around you. People-watching will tell you what style you like and what style you don't like. My passion for fashion started at fourteen years old reading magazines and studying the fashion the models wore. Even now, from time to time, I'll pick up a *Style* magazine at the checkout of the grocery store. However, we don't have to be limited to just magazines. Now, because of the wonderful world of the internet, you can head over to Pinterest,

28 Ways to Make it a Choice to Have Great Style

Facebook, Instagram, and Twitter! Anyone we follow has the potential to enlighten us and teach us something, whether we realize it or not.

It's important to be intentional and put social media to good use with a style mentor. What's even better is to have several style mentors. The "going out on the town" style mentor, the churchgoing style mentor, the boss lady, and professional style mentor. Years ago, I didn't know the significance of good style for every occasion. I knew how to put a look together for date night with my "Big Daddy" (the term of endearment I gave my husband, Ray). I knew how to dress for church on Sundays, and black-tie events. However, in going out with friends or everyday life, I was lost. I will never forget going out to the club with a bright orange shaggy sweater on and not knowing how hot it can get in a club even in the winter months! I was in my early twenties and experimenting with new looks. I had on a wig, and between that shaggy sweater and the wig, I thought I'd pass out from heatstroke! Which is why I put emphasis on why many style mentors are essential for every style occasion. Here are a few of my personal style mentors: Katherine Hepburn, Jacqueline Kennedy, and Meghan Markle. I tend to sway towards timeless classic style, but I like to add at least one accessory that's offbeat to add to my uniqueness.

Create Your Own List of Fabulous Women Whose Style Inspires You:

1. ....
2. ....
3. ....
4. ....
5. ....

Success leaves clues, so use your style mentor to lead the way to inspiration to look your best!

CHAPTER 6

PERSONALIZE YOUR STYLE PERSONAL

STYLE IS NOT REASONED BY what you wear; it's the subtotal and essence of who you are. – Kanika Starr Reynolds

The previous CHAPTER spoke of the importance of a style mentor, but that's not to replace the need of personal style that you have to define for yourself. This is a guide, but it's not the "know all, be all." This book is a great success if it allows you to stir up creativity and discover some things about yourself that you never really considered before. We are not put on earth to be clones, so personal style is always the way to feel different in a world that tries to make us all the same. The wonderful world of fashion is an easy way to express yourself. It's also fun to be creative finding many ways to restructure an outfit. It is my hope that you embrace the many interesting things that patterns, jewelry, fabrics, and colors can reveal without saying a word. Don't be afraid to express who you are in unconventional ways. Style isn't just about clothes; it's about quiddity and essence, so don't put yourself in a box. Discovery is fulfilling. Pay attention to the thing that makes you come alive when you wear it or when you see it. Be a paradox with style; wear a feminine dress with a motorcycle jacket or pair polka dots with stripes. Style is what *YOU* make it, as long as it's comfortable for you. Switch the belt that comes with a jumpsuit with a different color belt to change up the look. Buy the big sunglasses to add mystery. Pair leather with lace. Just create a look that's yours. Individuality is key, so don't be afraid to take a risk if it's something that you love, even if it's a bit offbeat. Look back at different genres of style because you may want to incorporate the old with the new.

It's okay to be a maverick in fashion and paint outside of the lines. The woman who is comfortable with being herself will set herself apart from everyone else! Here are a few ideas to personalize your style.

- Try different types of hats.

- Try eyewear in different prints like leopard or in different shapes and colors.
- Try sunglasses that are bigger than you usually wear.
- Add a belt in a bold color.
- Tie scarfs different ways (YouTube is very helpful for a tutorial.)
- Try different types of accessories such as a flower, a pin, or a broach.

Style isn't about perfection, it's about uniqueness!

CHAPTER 7

BE A DIVA ON A DIME
(VINTAGE, FLEA MARKET, THRIFT)

The best part about being a diva on a dime is pulling a look together from various places without spending much and feeling fabulous when the look comes together. – Kanika Starr Reynolds

FIRST, LET ME ESTABLISH WHAT a diva is because it has several meanings. One meaning is a prima donna who is difficult to work with. That's not the meaning I want to discuss. The definition of a diva that I want to use in this context is a glamorous and successful female or personality. That is what your aim is, to be glamorous and successful. With that being said, you can indeed become a diva without breaking the bank, making you a diva on a dime! It's not about where you shop; it's about how you bring the look together! How I learned to be a diva on a dime was in high school when I started thrift shopping at Goodwill. It all came about because

I wanted to be different and curate my own style. I didn't have to worry about someone wearing the same dress as me because the chances of two of the same dresses being at Goodwill or even them shopping at Goodwill was slim to none. I would mix the latest trend with retro fashion and create the perfect blend of past meets present.

Looking back, I see eclecticism is where my style spawned. My shopping nowadays is comprehensive with vintage, designer, trends, classic, and even costumes for parties with a theme. Many of all those styles I find at Goodwill; some of my best-dressed moments came from there. Like buying a used car, the first buyer pays the most on the new car price. When the previous owner sells the car, it may have miles on it, but it's still good for the new owner. I admit, everything I wear is not secondhand because some things are so unique and fabulous that it calls my name even at full price in a department store! If I pay full price for something, I love it so much that I wear it often. If it's constantly being worn, it's worth it to pay full price if you love it and can afford it!

But I will be honest; it's hard for me to pay full price because clothes depreciate in value and I've found far too many Goodwill garments that I've felt fabulous in. The rule I use is to invest in classic pieces that will get multiple wear, and trendy apparel let the first owner pay the high price and you get it secondhand. Save your money for vacations, things that create memories, or better yet invest in things like real estate or making your personal dreams come true. Those things will make you money in the long run. Nobody has to know where it comes from or how much you spent on it, because you can have expensive clothes and no style and on the other hand, you can have inexpensive clothes with great style.

Diva on a on a dime tips

- Look the garment over thoroughly to make sure there are no holes or stains on it, and if it has a hole, is it worth the fix?
- Don't buy it just because it's inexpensive; only buy it if you love it and will wear it.
- Think of how many ways you can wear it.
- Look at the tag to know the value of what you're buying. Some garments can be bought brand new at the store if the store it came from is inexpensive.
- Check the tag to see if it's a dry-clean-only garment, and if so, consider how much

dry-cleaning would cost. I once bought my daughter a homecoming dress at Goodwill that was $6.36 and the dry-cleaning was $19.99, but the dress was a designer dress that would have cost hundreds of dollars at a department store.

- Does it need tailoring? If so, how much would alterations cost? Is it worth it to you if it's a $10 dress and it's $35 to get it tailored?

I personally don't mind sharing with people where I find my clothes. I share because maybe it can inspire someone to think outside of the box when it comes to shopping. It's also a reminder that we can look good no matter if we have little money or a lot of money. You may not feel as comfortable sharing your "diva on a dime" finds, and if that's the case, when someone compliments you, all you have to say is "thank you."

Here is a thought to ponder when thrift shopping: it doesn't matter where we got it if we feel fabulous in it!

CHAPTER 8

BECOME A GREAT SHOPPER

Shops often, buy sparingly. – Unknown

WHILE TALKING TO A FRIEND, she stated words I have never uttered out of my mouth. She boldly confessed that she hates shopping for clothes! She lets the mannequin pick out her clothes; what the mannequin wears, she buys. I couldn't believe what I was hearing. For sure, I thought that even if a woman bought clothes that they couldn't put together well, they still enjoyed looking for them! This was another life lesson for me that we are not all the same and what one woman considers a joy, another woman may loathe. Love of shopping has never been an issue for me, over-shopping, maybe, but not loathing it. I can shop for just about anything and enjoy it. However, after filing bankruptcy because of my struggle with delayed gratification, I learned ways to still do what I love without having buyer's remorse later.

Here's what I learned that has helped me become a great shopper.

Know what you already have and do inventory of what you need. Write a list on paper or in your phone; this way you will shop on purpose.

Stick to the list.

If it's a store, get acquainted with the sales clerk. Get on their email list and they'll inform you of upcoming sales.

Wear comfortable clothes and shoes while shopping. I like to wear a dress when I shop because one garment is easier to take off than layers.

Try on the clothes and think about what shoes will be worn with the selections you're shopping for. It may be a good idea to bring the shoe so you ensure it looks good with what you're shopping for. Bring various sizes to the dressing room because depending on the brand, your size can fluctuate. I start with a size bigger than what I usually wear and a size smaller than I wear, and if one size doesn't fit the other sizes are already in the dressing room.

Remember, size doesn't matter, fit does. If in doubt, ask the sales associate for her opinion. The salesperson is there to help.

Wear comfortable shoes while shopping, I can't stress this enough. You may need to go to several stores and hurt feet will make you hasty in a purchase just to go home and get out of your shoes.

Wear the undergarments or girdle that you will wear while wearing the clothes you're about to buy. Foundation is very important. Tuck it and smooth it, good foundation will also help with good posture.

If you have a particular designer you love, you probably already know your size. That makes it easier if you like to shop online.

Do splurge on quality pieces that you will wear often. Unless your bank account is boundless, it's wise not to spend a lot of money on the latest trend that will change quickly.

Have a budget. Although I suggested you splurge on quality pieces, always do research and have a budget when you shop. It's not fabulous to be in debt looking fabulous so have a budget set aside and stick to it.

Buy trendy pieces that are inexpensive to mix with basics and classics that you already have.

Last but certainly not least, BUY ONLY WHAT YOU LOVE! Your style is personal, so think about what you want it to say about you! If you love it, can envision yourself in it, it fits well, and you can afford it, buy it! It's a bad feeling to wait for a sale for a piece you can't stop thinking about only to go back for it and it's gone! If it speaks to your heart, take it home. The joy you get every time you wear it will be worth it!

Here's a list of essential chic pieces that make a firm foundation to your wardrobe:

1. Dark blue denim jeans
2. Cardigan (basic colors black, tan, white, gray, and leopard)
3. Kitten Heels (great for long periods of standing)
4. Black Flat Shoes
5. Little Black Dress
6. Black Pumps
7. Crisp White Button-Down Shirt

8. Black Fitted Slim Pants
9. Scarf
10. Statement Jewlery
11. Pencil Skirt
12. Sunglasses
13. Trench Coat (Black, Tan, or Red)
14. Quality Handbag (investment piece)
15. Black Tailored Suit (investment piece)
16. Quality Belts (wide and skinny)
17. Pretty Pajamas
18. Tee Shirts
19. Tank Shirts
20. Spanx, girdles, and nice lingerie. You may be the only one who sees it, but you'll feel great knowing you're fabulous right down to your undies.
21. Good Fitting Swimwear
22. Signature Perfume
23. Convertible Bra
24. Nice Umbrella
25. Jean Jacket

Disclaimer, this entire list may not be for every woman. Style is personal, so being comfortable and being yourself is the epitome of style. Pick and choose what works for you.

CHAPTER 9

JEANS

Never underestimate the power of a good fitting pair of jeans. – Kanika Starr Reynolds

A GOOD FITTING PAIR OF jeans can come in handy for being cute while out and about. Jeans can be repurposed in many ways going from casual Friday at work to night out on the town with the girls after work. At work, a cute sleek blouse or a button-up shirt with a blazer and a pair of heels is a great way to still look fabulous for Friday when it's appropriate to dress down. This same look can also be transitioned into after-work attire. However, if you're feeling a little like you're still on the clock and you're meeting the girls after work, ditch the blazer and grab a cardigan. If the weather is cool, layer with a scarf, and roll up your jeans, you can also switch out of those heels and put on some oxfords for cute and comfort. A good rule of thumb is to get jeans in a darker wash because they are dressier and light-colored jeans are more casual. Look for a pair of jeans that isn't too tight and fits just right. They should be a little longer in length, the hem should end just a little past the ankle because this length works well with a pair of heels. If you really like the way the jeans fit, buy a second pair that is shorter in length to wear with flats.

Here are a few tips for the perfect pair of jeans:

Jeans should always flatter! Make sure that they fit in the waist, the legs, the butt, and the length. Saggy jeans are not flattering at all! If you're shorter than 5'2", look for jeans in petite and if you're 5'6" and taller, there are jeans especially for your height made for longer legs. The key to great style is always great fit, so if you see a jean that you really like and they may be too long, take them to the tailor and get them tailored to fit you to perfection.

The boyfriend jean is perfect for a Saturday grocery shopping or running errands. I love to pair them with a white V-neck T-shirt because it can be worn universally with so many fun pieces, but your favorite graphic shirt will make it all the more fabulous showing a little personality. Another avenue to wear the boyfriend jeans is with a tee and a leather jacket or even a sweater with heels or Converse sneakers to give a little street style.

The ripped jeans has transcended a trend and has become an integral part of the modern woman's wardrobe. Who would have thought we'd pay money to wear jeans that are bought with holes in them? We do and here are some suggestions on wearing them well. When dressing up the cut-up jean, the key is making something torn look intentional and cool. In the same way the dark denim and boyfriend jean is worn, this jean can be worn with a sweater, sweatshirt, tank top, graphic tee, turtleneck, or a button up. Add accessories and create different looks. If the boyfriend jeans or the ripped jeans aren't your favorite, also consider the boot-cut jean and wide leg.

The color of the jeans is also important. A dark denim gives a slimming affect and also can be dressed up. The lighter jeans are a little more casual. A white jean is polished and timeless for spring and summer. As mentioned, a nice flattering fit jean can also be worn to casual Friday at work (make sure management has made this attire permissible.).

Some styles should be worn leisurely at home or at play. Too much skin showing in any corporate setting is always a no-no, so to play it safe in the work place, save the cut-out jeans for play, not work.

Make sure to read the label of your favorite jeans when cleaning them. If it says wash jeans in cold wash and tumble dry, then do as it says. The right pair of jeans can be costly, but if you follow the rules on preserving them, they will keep you fabulous a long time. If you really find a pair that flatters your body shape, get them in different washes to customize a few different looks.

CHAPTER 10

THE BLACK DRESS

If there could only be one dress in your closet, it should be a well-fitted black dress because it can be worn many different ways.
– Kanika Starr Reynolds

THE LITTLE BLACK DRESS, ALSO universally known as the LBD, is a staple piece that should be in every woman's closet. It's versatile because of its neutral color. The LBD works for date nights, parties, funerals, and everything in between. There are many variations of the little black dress, so the dress you choose depends on the occasion it's needed. If there is a dress code on an invitation to an event, always follow the dress code. Here are a few occasions you may need to pull out a fabulous black dress from your closet or purchase a little black dress for an event:

Formal Black Dress

It's so fun to get glammed for a formal event. A reason to be a real-life Cinderella. When the invite says "formal" or "black tie" that usually means long dress and look your best! Many times it's for a wedding, balls, and even milestone birthdays. There will be lots of pictures and videos to capture special occasion moments so look good for your picture memories and for the host's memories as well. The details that go into the look of getting dressed for a formal event are just as important as the dress itself. The purse we carry should match the glitz of the dress. Never wear a work bag to a formal event. A clutch is always appropriate for formal occasions. Also, jewelry should be considered. If the neckline of the dress is high, then there should be no need for a necklace but play up the wrist with a beautiful bracelet. Drop-down bling earrings also compliment a formal dress well if the dress neckline is high. If a necklace is worn, it's good to match the earrings with the necklace or at least they should be similar. Shoes should be comfortable so it's easy to saunter around, so test them to make sure they are comfortable prior to the event. It looks bad to see a woman all dressed up but walking with a wobble because her shoes hurt her feet. Make sure your pedicure is fresh if you're wearing peep-toe shoes or opened-toe shoes. It's the details that make great style.

Cocktail Dress

The length of the cocktail dress is at the knee or above the knee. These dresses are fun to wear at a variety of parties. Many have embellishments and even feathers to add flair. Have fun with accessories and definitely wear a heel or a pump. The same rules apply with the purse, keep the workbag at home and carry a clutch and it's okay to add a little bling to the look. If the weather is cool, throw on a stole or a shawl.

Funeral Dress

Black may be the color the majority wears to a funeral but add a pop of color or a print. You can also add pearls or diamonds, whether pseudo or real. Hats and fascinators are an added appurtenance to your funeral look. It's not offending the deceased when we look our best laying them to rest.

Work Dress

Wearing black at work is appropriate. Leave the cocktail dresses for the parties and gowns for the weddings. Try not to look like you're headed to a funeral. If you have a black dress that can be layered, try adding a white button-up underneath; add a cardigan or a blazer. The key is to jazz up the mundane with a pop of color or an unexpected print. The little black dress can transition to be the cute work dress with a little creativity.

<u>Wrap Dress</u>

The wrap dress is elegance made simple. It is flattering to just about all shapes and sizes. You can accessorize with a belt or beautiful jewelry, and you're ready with confidence to enter any room!

As you can see, there are many ways and reasons to wear a black dress. This is one of those garments that I always look for when I'm at Goodwill thrift shopping. I have found many designer black dresses there. I know that for some reason or another, I will need black dresses so I have them already available for any occasion.

CHAPTER 11

SUNDAY BEST

On the third day, Esther put on her royal attire and stood in the inner court of the palace across from the king's throne. – Esther 5:1

I LOVE SUNDAYS BECAUSE BEING a hairstylist for more than twenty years, church gave me a reason to do what I didn't do at work—put on pretty clothes and feel like a lady getting all dressed up. Growing up, some of my fondest memories were of being a kid sitting next to my mom, admiring her all dressed up in her Sunday's best. She loves hats and would put on a dress or a two-piece skirt suit and finish the look with costume jewelry. I don't remember the sermons as a child, but I remembered sitting next to my fashionable mommy! Church has changed a lot over the years and we don't have to get dressed to the nines. In the church I attend now, it's not frowned upon to show up in ripped jeans and a flannel shirt. However, I still believe in Sunday's best when I enter the House of the Lord! I still love to get dressed up and come in my best. A dress, costume jewelry, heels, and sometimes even a hat like my mommy. I guess I'm my mother's child!

Here are a few tips to be appropriate at church and look your Sunday's best:

- Do a hand test on skirts and dresses. Put your hands at your side and if your fingertips are touching skin and not the garment, it's probably too short.
- Make sure it's not too much cleavage showing. If the dress cleavage is too low, put on a camisole to keep the look modest.
- If you wear pants, give them some slack. Super tight-fitting pants is not a good look for church.

The bottom line is the focus should be on God when we go to church and we should not distract other people from God because of inappropriate clothes that bring attention while at church.

CHAPTER 12

DATE NIGHT DRESSING

No matter how long you're in a romantic relationship or marriage, never stop dating, and when it's time to get dressed, dress to impress as if it's your very first date. – Kanika Starr Reynolds

AT THE TIME THIS BOOK is published, I will have been married twenty-two years. That is a lot of dates to get dressed up for and I love every minute of it. Aforementioned, I worked at a hair salon for more than twenty years and I wasn't wearing heels and skirts to work, so date night and church gave me a reason to dress up and feel fabulous. I would need pertinent information before getting my date night look together. It consisted of asking questions like, where are we going for date night and what will the weather be like while we're out? This will determine what is appropriate to wear. Maybe it's a game or dinner and a movie but whatever it is, you need to know so you can dress to impress and look your best. Whether it's a guy you just met, your fiancé/future husband, or your current husband, date nights should never end! Once you know the details, think cute and comfort. Casual is jeans, a tee, and a blazer, and if it's a game or an outdoor activity some cute white comfortable gym shoes. If it's dinner, a dress and some pumps can keep it chic but also simple. The key is to accessorize! The dress shouldn't be too tight or too short. In the words of Edith Head, "Your dress should be tight enough to show you're a woman but loose enough to show you're a lady!" Put effort into every date night. As you look your best, it will give you confidence and make your mate proud to be your side.

CHAPTER 13

THE STYLE SUCCESS FOR THE WORKING DIVA

Image on the job is just as important as knowledge of the job you're hired to do. – Kanika Starr Reynolds

YOU CAN WORK FOR YOURSELF, corporate, or a fast-food restaurant, but wherever you work, you not only represent yourself but you also represent that company! Imagine dining at a five-star restaurant and your server comes out and his clothes are dirty and his hair is disheveled. You more than likely would not want to eat there because your mind would think that if this business would allow a server to come out to serve patrons looking unkempt, then what in the world is the kitchen staff doing to the food? Image matters at every workplace. People will treat us how they perceive us. Carry yourself in a way that shows that you respect yourself and other people will respect you too. If you work at a company where uniforms are worn, always make sure the uniform is clean, pressed, and a belt is worn to help keep the look neat.

Length -

As mentioned in the previous CHAPTER, the length of the dress or skirt is important. Just like in high school, the workplace more than likely has a dress code in the hand manual and it's not really thought about until someone is called into the office for breaking it. The hand test applies for the work place just like when you were in school. If your fingers are touching skin when you put them at your side, the dress or skirt is too short. Do not distract with miniskirts. We can be fabulous and modest at the same time.

Cleavage -

It doesn't matter if your bra cup size is an A or DD, cover cleavage appropriately. Invest in a good bra and get fitted professionally so that your breasts are lifted up and covered. The right bra will keep bra bulge from showing lumps in your shirt and will make clothes fit better and look better. If a shirt is low and shows cleavage, then have different color camisoles in neutral colors like black, white, tan, and blue to wear underneath.

Bare Arms -

In most jobs in corporate America, it's considered appropriate to wear shirts or dresses showing bare arms in the workplace, but make sure there are no side boobs hanging. I actually prefer to wear a tailored blazer or a colorful cardigan to keep it professional. A rule of thumb is if the blazer or cardigan is printed or bold in color, the dress or pant should be demure or solid print. Sometimes, a pop of color is just enough. Other times monochromatic may be the look you're going for, depending on how you feel. Both are fabulous if you feel fabulous in it!

Shoes -

The size of the heel is important at work. Heels should be no higher than three inches. No sandals and no flip-flops; leave those for the beach and not the job. It's perfectly okay to have some taller heels in the car if you're leaving work and going out right after. Be ready for the after party after the 9-to-5. Shoes should always be in good condition.

Shoes really do tell a lot about a person. Remember that style is all about the details.

Here are a few staples to have in the closet to mix and match work attire:

- Blazer in black, camel, beige, or navy
- Trench coat in black, tan, or red
- Crisp white shirt
- Black tailored fit slacks
- Pencil Skirt
- Perfect fit sheath dress (black, beige, red, or navy)
- Pump in nude and black (kitten heel or no more than three-inch heel for work)

Keep hair nice and neat.

Keep nails manicured.

Makeup should be modest so they can hear what you're saying and not focus so much on the colors on your face. No rainbow shadows please, keep your makeup look neutral.

Be mindful of perfume, what smells good to you can be offensive to other people, so spray light.

If you're interviewing, make sure to always look professional. No halter tops, sundresses, or jeans. When you're hired in, no halter tops, sundresses, and only wear jeans if or when it's permitted.

You represent yourself, so give good representation. Carry yourself in a respectful way at all times.

CHAPTER 14

SLEEP PRETTY

Good dreams can come true in pretty pajamas. - Kanika Starr Reynolds

AS A WOMAN THERE ARE many things that make me feel like a lady. One is putting on pretty pajamas at night after a bubble bath or a hot shower. Silk or satin pajamas feel amazing after a long day. Many times we don't even know the stress that we've picked up from all of the busyness of the day and this is a simple way to unwind after a long day. Style doesn't turn off, even at night. It's about all of the things, accessories, details, and even the ambiance of an environment that make a woman feel beautiful. If for whatever reason silk or satin is not your preferred fabric for lounge wear, then a matching cotton pajama set will make you feel pretty too.

Another way to fall asleep pretty is a nighttime regimen. It's a great way to relax and clear your mind because beauty is not only about outside looks but inner emotions and a healthy mentality as well. Being a lady of class takes work. There are things that you can do intentionally to remind you that you're not just a woman but you're a lady. A lady cares about her image not just to the outside world but in the privacy of her own home. Wearing pretty pajamas, putting on a nice bathrobe after a bath, and relaxing your thoughts so you can be refreshed for the next day, will help you conquer your world the next day. If you haven't given much thought to what you wear at night, start to consider it. If you've been sleeping in old T-shirts and sweatpants, step it up a notch. I love places like TJ Maxx, Marshalls, and Ross for inexpensive night wear. Invest in yourself and sleep pretty.

Tips to remember to optimize the best night's sleep:

- Some women protect their hairstyles at night with a bonnet or headscarf. If you are a woman who wears either at night, keep them clean by washing them regularly. Keep in mind headscarves can also be cute. Get a few in solid colors that match your pajamas.

- Moisturize your body with scents that you enjoy, even if you sleep alone, smell lovely for yourself.
- Wash your sheets regularly and spray linen spray on them for a fresh scent.
- Make your bed up every morning.
- Keep your room free from clutter; style is also about the environment that we create.
- Play soft, relaxing music such as jazz or classical to prepare your environment for rest.
- Take a shower or bath at night, you'll sleep better.
- Lotion or Vaseline your feet and put on socks to protect your feet against dryness.

Before you go to sleep, turn off your mind and focus on the life you envision as your best life. I pray God gives you dreams at night that give you strategy to do it and become it.

Sweet dreams.

CHAPTER 15

TRAVEL FABULOUS

SOME PEOPLE LOVE TO TRAVEL and some people don't. I happen to love to travel; there have been many times that I've packed a backpack to save money on baggage fees, keeping the flight cheap for a much-needed weekend getaway (two- or three-night stay somewhere.) I'm proud of myself for the roll-up clothing technique I've learned and how I can mix and match putting many days' worth of clothes in a twenty-inch suitcase.

Here are a few tips I've learned that may help you:

The first thing to do is check the weather. There's no point in packing heavy clothes for hot weather. Look in your closet for transitional pieces that will transform from day to night. Neutral colors work great as building blocks to go along with a few bold pieces. A nice pair of denim jeans or trousers, a V-neck T-shirt, a blazer or a cardigan, and a scarf can be stylish while on the plane but all of those pieces can be worn differently throughout the trip. It's also good to wear all heavy clothing on the plane. The scarf is great to wrap around you on the plane because sometimes the aircraft is cold. Also, decide what activities you'll do on the trip. Even business trips may leave time for personal pleasure in the evenings. Will you dress up for dinner? What about a swim? Consider this while packing. It's better to have them and not need them than to need them and not have them.

Here are things to remember while packing:

Lay out all clothes that you plan to take three days prior to traveling and glance them over the day before. There may be some changes to your choices. Is there anything that can be worn more than once? The plan is to pack light because luggage costs money to carry on a plane and there are weight limits to the luggage and you never know what you may find shopping while you're there.

Take a picture in a full-length mirror to remember how you paired the look together with jewelry.

Remember a first aid kit.

Remember your passport if traveling internationally.

Spring/Summer Packing:

Sun hat - Fedora or wide brim, just make sure it can be packed without getting flat. The shape of the hat is important. You can also carry it in hand if it's wide and won't fit in your luggage.

Beach flip-flops - That you don't mind getting wet or sandy.

Swimsuits and swimsuit cover-ups

A pair of jeans (white jeans always look chic in the summer)

Light cardigan for cooler air in the evening or if air is on. Cardigans also look great over sundresses.

Dresses: They're easy to roll up in your luggage and a complete look all by themselves. Think airy and light. Don't be afraid to bring a dress with prints; it looks chic. Place plastic between dresses to help prevent wrinkles.

Sandals: Sandals - That you can dress up. Patent leather and jewels take a casual sandal from ordinary to extraordinary, and cute sandals are a must. Make sure they're in good condition. Sandals would make a good investment piece because summer after summer they get worn. Make sure to get a fresh pedicure when toes are out.

Comfortable Walking Shoes: These shoes can be the same shoes worn on the plane. Tennis shoes have come a long way and many can be worn with dresses too. If they are new, walk around in them to see if they are comfortable for substantial amounts of time.

Heels: One pair will suffice. It's good to have a neutral pair that can be worn from day to night with whatever you've packed.

Sunglasses: Sunglasses have a purpose to keep sun out of our eyes, but they are also instant glam. Try on many pairs to get the right frame that compliments your face shape. Then don't leave home without them, let me remind you again, sunglasses are instant glam.

Clutch Purse: a small bag is perfect for dinner without carrying a beach bag or your everyday purse. It takes up little space in the suitcase and can double as a jewelry bag, placing your travel jewelry pieces inside (if jewelry is of value or expensive, keep it in your carry-on with you to protect it.)

Packing for Fall/Winter is a little different and here are a few things to consider:

- Sweater
- Jeans
- White collar shirt
- Blazer

Remember to wear a jacket or coat, jeans, and chunky sweaters on the plane because those are items that take up space. Also, boots or shoes that are heavy should be worn while traveling because they, too, can take up unnecessary space in the luggage.

Another thing to think about for traveling fabulous is making sure your luggage is sturdy and stylish. Luggage says a lot about the traveler. It doesn't have to be designer, but it can definitely be cute. I've found fabulous luggage at places like TJ Maxx and even Ross Dress for Less. There's no excuse to not look chic for a weekend getaway or boarding the plane.

Don't forget to look for pieces at the local market or boutiques to enhance your wardrobe when traveling. What you choose should always speak to your style. It may be a unique scarf or a tribal necklace, but wearing a keepsake or memorabilia from your travels will bring beautiful memories all over again from that experience.

CHAPTER 16

PURSES, HAND BAGS, AND OTHER BAGS

A handbag tells a lot about the woman; it has all of our necessities in it. Make sure it represents you well. - Kanika Starr Reynolds

THERE ARE MANY THINGS THAT a woman can't have enough of and many would attest that shoes and purses are two of them. There are many types of purses a woman should have for the many occasions that she has to wear them. The purse we carry depends on the woman who carries it. One thing every woman should consider is that the purse we carry everyday should not only be pretty but practical. Some women carry small bags for only the essentials like keys, lipstick, and phone. Other women carry big bags and they have everything but the kitchen sink in there (all jokes aside, I'm that woman.) This woman is afraid that she may need something and not have it, so her purse is a mini warehouse to house snacks, a full makeup bag, sunglasses in the case, travel-size air freshener, and everything in between. A behemoth bag requires organization. I pick up small clear plastic makeup bags and organize my snacks, stationery, makeup, and feminine products so that everything is together and not loose at the bottom of the bag. Compartmentalizing things in clear bags saves time; a woman of style has no time to waste looking for things, but she knows where they are because of organization. If you carry a big bag, decide what is necessary to have in the bag because years of carrying weight on the shoulders can in time cause pain in your shoulders and back. Keep your purse clean and organized so you're not carrying more weight than you need to (this can also apply to our life.)

There are many different types of purses that a fabulous woman should have. Here are a few to have in your closet:

Everyday Bag - It's just as it says, made for every day. I've said it before but let me reiterate: it should be cute and stylish but also practical. Since this bag is used daily it should be durable and easy to keep clean because it gets much use and the goal is to stay fabulous, always.

Work Bag - Your work bag is different than an everyday bag. It can be the bag that you only carry to work. Maybe it has more compartments in it to place snacks or it's wider so you have space to carry things like mints to go in your candy dish or maybe it has room for your laptop computer.

Clutch - this bag is for dinner dates, parties, or special occasions. A clutch bag is a feminine bag that adds detail to a total glam look. It's usually small and dainty. Don't be afraid to let this small accessory bring a big bang to any special occasion. Remember the size when you think of the needs for the night. If the clutch isn't big enough for your phone, and your phone is a need, then find a bigger clutch.

Cross-body/Messenger - Great for travel because it keeps the purse in front of you and close to you; it's smaller in size and hands free. I also love to carry my cross-body when I grocery shop. Strap it across the body and keep it moving.

Travel Weekend Bag - This bag is big enough to put a change of clothes in, carry necessities that would be in a purse, and even a laptop for work. It's a multipurpose bag. It should be durable but also stylish.

Wallet - A wallet may be inside of the purse, but it still needs to be fabulous when it's pulled out. Throw away old receipts, papers, and transfer coins that create bulges to the coin jar in the house. A wallet should be able to zip or button with ease. If the wallet is worn, then get a new one. It's the details that make a woman fabulous, and although the wallet may not get a lot of showoff time when it is seen, when you pay for a purchase, it will show you're together right down to the accessory.

Do you know what's in your purse? Fabulous is order. Think about the things that are in your purse. Do they actually have need or is it just taking up space? Here are a few suggestions that should be in your purse:

- Kleenex
- Hand Sanitizer
- Phone
- Gum/Mints
- Powder Compact with a mirror
- Lipstick or gloss
- Travel-size air spray

A small book to read when you have to wait. We don't have to mindlessly scroll on the internet,

28 Ways to Make it a Choice to Have Great Style

be intentional about what goes in the mind with the book we read if we have to wait.

A lady carries a purse. Having the right purse for the right occasion shows refinement and class. A purse is an investment piece that is well worth it!

CHAPTER 17

SHOES

Give a girl the right pair of shoes and she can conquer the world. – Marilyn Monroe

ONE OF THE KEY INGREDIENTS to great style is great shoes. We can build an entire outfit around a great pair of shoes, and the wrong shoes, even with the right clothes, can abolish the whole look. I recommend to dress from the shoe up. Shoes make great conversation starters and a great conversation can open doors. Be intentional about the shoes you wear and make sure they're in good condition. Shoes can be one of the first things a person will look at when they see us and that's why I deem good-quality shoes an investment. There are many different types of shoes for many different reasons and occasions.

Here are a few shoe types that made my list:

Flats/ Ballerina – These shoes are great for travel or when there is a lot of walking but you still want to be fashionable and comfortable.

Peep-Toe – The peep-toe shoe shows the peep of the toe; it's a feminine shoe. Great for dinner or a date night out because it's sexy.

High Heel – It's great to have a couple pairs of high heel shoes in neutral colors. It's also great that this shoe is a classic that can be worn from day to night. Make sure the heel is comfortable to walk in. There's nothing classy about a woman that does not know how to walk in high heels, especially when she can choose the heel height most comfortable for her to walk in. Remember that if you love a shoe and the heel is too high, a shoe cobbler can cut the heel down.

Kitten Heel – The kitten heel is a great shoe if you have to go somewhere and there is a lot of walking or standing but you still want to wear a heel and be comfortable. I think it's also great for long hours at the office or any job where you have to stand a lot. It's also a great shoe when you've had problems with your knees or legs and wearing high heels is uncomfortable.

Boots – A tall leather boot in black, camel, or brown is great to have for instant style when wearing a dress, skirt, or jeans in the fall and winter seasons.

Tennis Shoes – Even during exercise or comfort, a stylish woman looks good. The right pair of tennis shoes can be stylish if you find the right fit, color, and style. If you choose white tennis shoes, keep them white and clean. It's never stylish to wear dirty shoes. If the white tennis shoes are too much upkeep, then go for black tennis shoes so the dirt isn't so easily seen.

The maintenance of shoes that we wear is just as important as the shoe itself. Keep shoes polished and shined; taps and soles should be in good condition; and shoes should be free from scuffs and markings. A great shoe can go a long way with any ensemble.

Kanika's Life Changing Shoe Shopping Experience

This is the boot for a girl like you!

I can remember it like it was yesterday; although it was many years ago, I never forgot it. I walked into Macy's looking for a riding boot to be comfortable and chic for one of my yearly travels to the Bronner Brother's Hair Show in Atlanta. I knew my new boots needed to be black and tall, but I didn't know going to buy them would be a lesson I'd use throughout my life. Looking at the riding boots, I picked up a pair of Calvin Klein's. A salesman, whose name I can't remember, came over to me and said, "You're not a Calvin Klein girl. You're a Cole Haan girl!" I never put much thought into Cole Haan until then, and after I tried on a pair of tall, all-black, "genuine leather from bottom to top" boots, I knew that was the boot to invest in.

The boots were hundreds of dollars more than the first pair I picked up, but there was something about them that spoke to my spirit. The fit could have been tailored just for me, the leather was quality, they had a Nike insole, and my strut felt like I was on a runway when I walked in them. I'm not sure if the guy said that to get a higher commission, but whatever the reason, I never forgot the level-up lesson he taught me. I learned to buy the best you can afford and walk away feeling like the purchase was worthy. I still have those Cole Haan boots and I still feel fabulous wearing them.

CHAPTER 18

BASIC ETIQUETTE

*"Good manners are made up of petty sacrifices." –
Ralph Waldo Emerson*

STYLE IS ALSO ABOUT SOPHISTICATION. We've seen women who look put together on the outside, but when they open their mouth, they curse or talk about other people showing a lack of class and refinement. The best way to remember to use manners and etiquette is to practice at home when there is no audience. Simple things that make us better can be practiced in privacy when no one knows we're practicing. I practice getting out of the car like a lady when I run my errands; I practice the tone of my voice at home; and I also practice being a better listener and not making the conversations all about me. Mistakes are better when they are made in private. What we continue to do becomes a habit and the goal is to practice good habits all of the time, every day.

28 Ways to Make it a Choice to Have Great Style

Here are a few simple tips on etiquette, which is quintessential to class and great style.

1. Manners – We were taught this at a very young age, but it must be reiterated. The words *please*, *thank you*, and *you're welcome* will always be appropriate. Use them often.

2. Dress to impress – It doesn't seem fair, but people treat us how they perceive us. Before we say a word, we've already been judged by how we look. This doesn't mean everywhere we go we have to dress to the nines, but it does mean wherever we go, we should look our best and appropriate for the occasion. If you're unsure of how to dress for a particular occasion, then YouTube it or google it. We should carry ourselves like we care about ourselves and that will teach other people how to treat us too.

3. Conversation – make sure conversation is pleasant. We never want to be a gossip. Not only because we don't want the gossip to get back to them but gossiping about people is wrong and shows a lack of class. In the words of Eleanor Roosevelt, "Great

minds discuss ideas; average minds discuss events; small minds discuss people." Don't be a small mind. When we go out, it's great to network and meet new people, learn about them, and share a little about yourself to make sure the conversation is mutual. Weigh your words and if the other party has few words to share and there's awkward silence, fill the silence with a genuine concerned question, about them. Another rule of thumb is to know when to pull out your cell phone. When dining at a restaurant, the people at your table should not have to compete with social media, so divert all eyes on who is conversing with you. A few pictures are okay to capture the memory but save the photo shoot for after the experience. Take it all in, enjoy the moment, and the fulfillment of mutual stimulating conversation.

4. Check your volume and tone – Being too loud is rude. It shows and comes across as one who is ostentatious. The goal is to make them want to lean an ear and come closer because you appear to be interesting and they want to hear what you have to

say. Don't let them down. Tell a memorable story but make it concise as you can without leaving the most memorable details out and please use your inside voice while doing so.

5. If you're at a party or gathering, you don't have to make a grand adieu when you leave. Let the hostess know you're leaving and make it brief. He/she has other guest to entertain so make sure the goodbye doesn't make a scene and lead other guests to leave behind you.

6. Table Manners – Just a few table manners to think about. There are many more, but these are some of the most common. Never eat with elbows on the table. Silence cell phones and put them away. Dab your mouth with a napkin, don't wipe. If you know what restaurant you're eating at beforehand, get familiar with the menu so there's no holdup when it's time to order. If dining with other guests, wait until all meals are brought to the table before you start to eat, unless the person or people waiting says otherwise.

7. If you're invited to someone's home, always bring a hostess gift. The hostess took the

time to prepare a gathering and took the time to invite you, so the least you can do is bring a candle, bottle of wine, or even a book of inspiration.

Style is more than dress; it's everything about you. Practice good etiquette so when in public you're a class act.

CHAPTER 19

DRESS FOR YOUR AGE

It's tasteless to try and hold on to the days of our youth with an image that we should have grown out of. – Kanika Starr Reynolds

YOU'VE HEARD IT SAID, "DRESS your age, not your shoe size." Well, there is truth to that statement! What worked in your twenties won't work in your forties; what worked in your forties won't work in your sixties; you're not that same woman. Body shapes change and even personalities can change from decade to decade, so why wouldn't our style of dress change as well? Besides great-fitting clothes, one of the most important style choices we can make as a woman of class is dress appropriately for our age. It is tasteless to see a mature woman wear immature clothes. The older we get, the classier we get. We want to be taken seriously, so we dress like it. We are no longer shopping in the junior section. Anywhere you go, you should feel confident and be respected and that starts with your image. This confidence is about being polished both inside and out.

I personally believe that as we get older dressing should become easier. We don't want to spend a whole lot of time deciding what we will wear because everything in our closet should be sleek and presentable to wear no matter where we go. If you have to go to the office, then you should look chic or if you have to make a grocery store run, then you should still look put together. One way to simplify dressing is making sure only what fits well and is fabulous is in your closet. Another way to keep it simple is to buy classic pieces but show personality with nice jewelry. This jewelry can be custom jewelry or jewelry that you've invested in such as a diamond bracelet, pearls, stacking rings, and a beautiful watch.

In your twenties

Sartorially, in your twenties, it's perfectly fine to be adventurous with your style. If you want to mix stripes and polka dots because that's what you're feeling, go for it. Leopard tights, go for it; just make sure you're comfortable in it! There's far less judgment during this time because you're figuring out what you like, who you are, and having fun as you find out. You're young and free to express yourself!

In your thirties

In our thirties, we make some changes to our image because we're more established. Many women have children in school and we do not want to embarrass them when we go to conferences to meet the teacher! There's room for some clothing risk, but keep it at a minimal because you want to be taken seriously and respected.

In your forties

You should know who you are, what you like and don't like, and be okay if nobody else likes you because you like you. You've experimented with all kinds of trends and now you've tailored a style that best fits you and the image you desire for yourself.

In your fifties and beyond

Classic and simplified. It shouldn't take all day to get dressed because you have key staples and quality pieces that are fabulous and tailored for your style. Less is more. It's all about the details and there should be one, no more than two statement pieces that you wear daily, like a necklace or a belt that shows a tad of unique style. Hair should be coiffed, hands are manicured, and natural makeup will show how elegant and well put together you are. You may be getting older but your style will be timeless.

CHAPTER 20

WORTHY WORKOUT WEAR

The first wealth, is health. – Ralph Waldo Emerson

WE LIVE IN A WORLD that is engulfed in outward beauty but what good is outward appearance if the inside body is not healthy? That is why it's essential to exercise the body. Exercise can be taking the stairs instead of the elevator; parking farther in the parking lot to get more steps in; taking a stroll around the neighborhood; and it can also mean going to the gym to workout. It's the latter that I'd like to talk about. If you are a woman that goes to the gym, remember that the gym is a public place, and whenever a woman is in public, she needs to look her best. That includes the clothes she wears to the gym while working out. Exercise is not a license to look a mess. Make sure that workout wear fits appropriately, you're matching the set, your sports bra fits properly, and your shoes are in good shape. Yoga and workout pants should fit so that they're not too tight or too big. If you have long hair a cute ponytail will keep hair out of your face. If you have short hair, a scarf that matches your workout clothes is a small investment to keep your hair together and to look good even when you sweat. Small stud earrings are appropriate but avoid big hoop earrings or gaudy jewelry.

It's also a good idea to get at least a week's worth of workout clothes so that you don't have to wash them as often. Read the machine wash labels so gym clothes can be washed correctly to keep certain materials from souring because some fabrics are made to hold moisture and that can make them smell bad.

There are many stores to find nice and stylish workout attire without breaking the bank. Places like Target, Ross Dress for Less, TJ Maxx, and even Sam's Club may have fashionable workout gear so you can look good as you get fit.

CHAPTER 21

ACCESSORIZE, ACCESSORIZE, ACCESSORIZE

STYLE IS IN THE DETAILS and the best way to have great style is to choose your accessories wisely. – Kanika Starr Reynolds

It is said that accessories should be seventy percent of our wardrobe. I couldn't agree more. Two different women can have on the same dress but accessorize it differently and the accessories can make all of the difference! There are so many accessories to choose from and that may be the reason so much of our wardrobe depends on them. There are so many ways to accessorize a look, but the key is not to have on all of your accessories at once. Select a few key pieces to make your look unique. What do you want your look to say about you? Once you know that, then let the scarf, necklace, or bevy of any other personal accessories do all of the talking. Here are a few of my favorite accessories that I like to use to dress up an ordinary look and make it extraordinary:

Scarf – there are many ways to accessorize the scarf. You can put it around your neck, wear it as a belt, or tie it in your hair. It can be dressed up casual for colder seasons or a short silk scarf around the neck can dress up a sheath dress or a white button-up shirt.

Belts – Instant chic to a dress is a nice belt. Play with the colors and the prints. A little black dress with a leopard print belt and you're ready for a date night or the boardroom. Think outside of the box; we don't have to limit the belt to a sheath dress. A belt also looks amazing over a cardigan, jumpsuit, jacket, and even a sweater. When worn over a sweater or anything that could be bulky, be mindful that the middle doesn't gather too much. The goal is to always look chic.

Statement Jewelry – The bling necklace, cuff bracelet, and chandelier earrings we wear can start a conversation that opens doors and build new relationships. These pieces of jewelry have the name "statement piece" for a reason. It can dress up the simplest of clothes. Putting on statement jewelry can even make jeans and a T-shirt look chic.

Bracelets – Bare arms deserve bracelets. The everyday bracelet can be sterling silver or gold, but it's a quick way to add pizzazz to an everyday look. When going out at night, add some bling around your wrist. If during the day and you're wearing pearls, a pearl bracelet will complete a look. Also note that bracelets can be double stacked and silver and gold can be mixed to create a unique look of your own.

Stockings/Tights/Socks – Style is in the details and the right leg wear can add flavor to a simple ensemble. Stockings should match your skin tone and make sure to carry a second pair just in case you get a run. Tights are a little different than stockings and are great for fall and winter because they're thicker. Stockings with print can be fun, but it's a good look to keep the dress you wear simple if the tights are busy in design. Also, keep tights classic in one color for work so you always look professional.

Hats – Hats are not only for "bad hair" days but for showing off pizzazz and personality. There are many hats a woman can wear. A cute fascinator looks great with a dress for a wedding. For a nice casual look, try the fedora with a pair of jeans and a T-shirt. A wide-brim hat is a stylish statement all by itself. Hats are fun; just make sure you're confident wearing it.

Gloves – Gloves are not just for winter wear. Try on a pair of formal gloves with a formal dress to add Marylyn Monroe glam or a pair of short gloves with a dress worn for church. It will bring back the vintage look of the early 1900s.

Reading/Eye Glasses – Glasses are a great way to show impeccable style. The shape of the glasses should complement the shape of your face (if you don't know the shape of your face, then google different face shapes and find yours because certain glasses and some hairstyles suit different face shapes better than others.) It's okay to experiment with eyeglasses in different colors and prints, such as leopard or zebra. Glasses are an investment because they're worn often. Anything that is worn often is good to invest in so that you can stay fabulous all of the time.

Sunglasses – Sunglasses are an instant way to look chic and glam. If you don't know what's the best sunglass shape for your face, then look at images of women who have your face shape and that will give you an idea of what would look best on you. Remember that sunglasses can be worn year round; if you live wear it snows in the winter there may be a glare that can be bright, so rock your sunglasses and be stylish all year round.

Umbrella – We don't have to be bummed because of the rain. Incorporate a coordinating umbrella to match outerwear and make the weather work for you as you turn heads because you're a class act, right down to your umbrella.

Rain Boots – I would consider rain boots an accessory because you are intentional about your style when you wear stylish rain boots and if they coordinate with a rain jacket, you'll get looks for being the best dressed woman in the rain.

Phone Case – You probably didn't expect a phone case to be part of the accessory list, but in this day and age because the phone is so essential to our everyday life, it made the list. A cell phone is used practically every day and the added detail of a fashionable phone case gives the woman carrying it a modicum of class.

Writing Pen – The small details matter, so when you pull out a pen to take notes and it's a beautiful color, print, or monogrammed it speaks class and attention to even the slightest detail. Same with a nice journal if you like to write. Match the pen and journal for an added touch.

Flower Pin – Only by experience can I tell you the difference a huge black flower pin has made in my wardrobe. My sister April (whom I affectionately call Sissy) gave me an artificial flower pin that is definitely a statement piece. I've worn it on the lapel of a blazer, in the middle of a bandeau dress, and it can even be a hair accessory. It is the only statement piece I wear when I have it on because nothing else has to compete for its attention.

Brooch – If a big flower pin is a bit ostentatious, then an ornamented brooch is another great accessory for the lapel of a blazer or sweater. Many may think of our grandmother when we see the word *brooch*, but style is all about rebirthing the classics and making them up to date. I was given a diamonique brooch with a crown, reminding me that I am a child of God and He is the King of Kings so that makes me feel like His princess. A brooch is a small detail that packs a big punch to being fabulous.

I've given you a few ways to be creative and stylish with accessories. Have fun getting dressed because finding the right look is fun. Select the right accessories because it's all about the details.

CHAPTER 22

SKIRTS

A fabulous skirt can give instant confidence to walk into any room, and own it. –Kanika Starr Reynolds

AS A WOMAN, WEARING A dress and heels is an instant way to feel like a lady, but there's something about wearing a skirt that brings out the girly side of us or the sophistication in us. A skirt is versatile and feminine and comes in many different styles. Let's go over a few popular skirts that can be key to your essential wardrobe.

Pencil Skirt: Have an important meeting? The pencil skirt can give a look of power and confidence and will look good on most figures. Don't be afraid to wear this skirt in a bold color to be chic in an instant.

A-line skirt: Another popular skirt that compliments many shapes is the A-line skirt. This skirt looks great for those with a pear-shaped body type because it covers the hips and will make the waist look smaller.

Wrap skirt: Is exactly how it sounds; wrap it around your waist and there's elegance effortlessly. The wrap skirt can be dressed up or down and can be short or long in length.

Tutu skirt: This skirt is fun to wear and must be worn in confidence because it grasps the attention of the onlooker for its boldness and drama. All by itself this skirt is a conversation piece and can be worn by fashionable women who are confident wearing it. If you like to go to an event and be elusive and humble, this is probably not the skirt to wear. I've worn this skirt with a T-shirt, leopard-print belt, and a matching leopard print clutch and cage high heels. I talked to just about everyone at the party because it was an interesting outfit and I was confident wearing it!

These are just a few of my favorite skirts. The most important thing is that the skirt you choose fits you well and that you are comfortable and confident in it.

CHAPTER 23

OUTERWEAR FOR THE OUTDOORS

The outerwear you wear says a lot about you so be cute while staying warm. – Kanika Starr Reynolds

OUTERWEAR IS ONE OF THE most worthwhile investment pieces that you can buy. If you live in a climate that's cold, you'll get your money's worth out of having a stylish and quality coat. Growing up in Michigan, I knew firsthand about outerwear. Be it trench coat, cape, leather jacket, or a down jacket, I've worn them all and they've been a great way to be fashionable in the winter season. Let's go over a few ways to look hot, even when it's cold outside.

The belted trench – The belted trench is a classic staple that can be worn all year round. It's a great way to flatter the waistline and it looks great over turtlenecks and collared shirts. The trench coat is versatile; it can be worn over a cocktail dress or with jeans and a T-shirt. It can also go from day wear to night wear. This coat is a staple that will never go out of style. Most can be worn as a raincoat as well because many are waterproof. The key is to be mindful of the fit. Make sure it's tailored and the garments worn underneath are smooth and not bulky. Go for a classic color like black, beige, or red so you get the maximum use out of it. The trench coat is definitely one of my top picks for a must-have stylish coat.

Leather Motorcycle Jacket – A leather jacket is a timeless staple that can easily transition a look from day to night. It can be worn with a pair of jeans or layered over a summer dress in the fall. It's a great way to mix a soft feminine look with edginess to make great paradoxical style.

Jean Jacket – I love a casual jean jacket, but most of the time I don't wear it with jeans. I love to wear a jean jacket with all black or over a sundress when it's cool outside. It's another jacket that can get a lot of use from day to night.

Raincoat – A stylish raincoat may not be a necessity in your closet, but I believe it's an added bonus to being intentional about looking fabulous.

When a woman checks the weather to know how to dress and shows up prepared, it says that you stay ready and rain won't keep you from looking stylish.

Blazer – A blazer may be a surprise to the list but when the temperature drops just a little, it can replace a lightweight jacket and look fabulous paired with a scarf. This outerwear should have a nice tailored fit or a looser fit for a casual look. A blazer can also be worn with jeans and a T-shirt, a dress, or a button-up shirt with slacks.

Anorak – The anorak jacket does not get enough credit for casual cuteness. I love this jacket because it's great for throwing on a little added warmth when you go to the gym or even if you want to layer it over a turtleneck. It's a fun spin on outerwear. Known for being casual, this jacket is also a transitional piece that can be worn with skinny jeans or a dress.

Cape – Instant glamour is the cape. Great for a dress-up occasion or jeans and boots. The cape outerwear is a sure way to show up fabulous. Superheroes may be fictitious, but you'll feel like real royalty wearing a cape.

28 Ways to Make it a Choice to Have Great Style

The right outerwear can make an outfit that was thrown together look like you're put together! It's not like a shirt that you wear every once in a while; what is worn outside gets worn over and over again, so make sure it's fabulous and has great style.

CHAPTER 24

WHEN TO SPLURGE AND WHEN TO SAVE

Great style is about mixing high-end fashion with inexpensive trends that make a total look that's your own. – Kanika Starr Reynolds

IN CHAPTER EIGHT, I GAVE a list of some essential pieces that a fabulous woman should own. This CHAPTER is about what pieces should be investment pieces and what you can get without breaking the bank (many of the items in CHAPTER 8 will be in this list.) What determines if the garment is worth the splurge is how much you will use it and how many times you will wear it. For instance, if a handbag costs $365 and you wear it every day for a year, it's one dollar a day. Now imagine keeping that bag in pristine condition and still wearing it for five, ten, or maybe even twenty years! When you keep it for a long time and it still looks good, you may not mind spending

$365, which is why it becomes an investment! I've compiled a list of the items I think are worth spending the money to purchase because they will be staples in your closet and you'll have them and use them for a very long time! On the other hand, I've made another list of what you can get from H&M or other inexpensive retailers at a fraction of the cost of department stores.

Splurge on these investment pieces (get the best that you can afford):

Jeans – A good pair of fitted jeans will help you to look slender and dress up any outfit from day to night. If you find a pair you really like, get two when they are on sale. One pair you can take to the tailor and get shortened so when you wear flat shoes or sandals, they will be the perfect length. Finding the right pair of jeans may not happen overnight. Take your time to find the perfect pair that you feel comfortable in.

Undergarments – A good-fitting bra for a woman who has big breasts will make your clothes look better. Get measured and pay the extra money for a good-fitted bra! Many women don't know the importance of a good-fitting bra and therefore what could have been a nice outfit, isn't noticed because the attention was on her badly fitting bra.

Pumps/heels – A good pair of pumps is priceless! It's a bad feeling to walk with hurt feet. Get the best high-heel pumps that you can afford because if you get them in a classic color, they will be timeless and last for many years.

White Button Collar Shirt – There's so much you can do with the white button-down collar shirt. I consider it an investment piece. The arm length and collar are both important details to a great white button-down shirt. This shirt can be dressed with jeans or a business suit when you go to a job interview or the office. It's a good idea to get this clothing staple dry-cleaned to keep it as crisp and white as possible.

Scarf – A nice scarf can be bought anywhere, but I do believe it's a good idea to invest in at least one designer scarf that you can afford. The scarf can be worn with clothes from inexpensive stores but will make the entire outfit look expensive.

Belt – A belt is another accessory that can take a look from ordinary to extraordinary (nice to have a reversible belt that gives both black and brown color). Belts can be worn around dresses, cardigans, and with pants. You'll get lots of use out of it and it will make the ensemble look polished and chic.

Sunglasses – A great pair of designer sunglasses is instant glam. Therefore, I consider them an investment.

Business Suit – Every woman if she works in corporate America, goes to interviews, or does public speaking of some sort, should invest in a quality business suit in a classic color (black, tan, or brown.) Make sure the fit is tailored to you so it looks upscale and polished. What's great is the blazer and slacks can be worn separately to switch up the look. Wear the blazer over a dress or wear the slacks with a printed shirt.

A Jacket or Coat – Definitely an investment to splurge on a fabulous jacket or coat. Outerwear gets worn over and over again, so you will look and feel fabulous by carefully choosing one you love of good quality and a great fit.

Purse/Handbag – I believe that the handbag a woman carries says a lot about her, so make sure yours is saying "I invest in the best." This by far should be one of the most important investment pieces in your wardrobe. The hardware of a handbag, the straps, and the leather should be of good quality. It doesn't have to be a known designer, but a bag that will last the test of time. Cheap purses and knockoffs may look appealing, but soon you'll have to buy another once the handles are frayed and the faux leather is peeling. There may be an upscale consignment store that you can find an authentic designer purse for less. Clothing usually depreciates in value, but some designer handbags actually appreciate in value and may be worth much more when it becomes vintage. Do your research and find the handbag that speaks to you not just the most popular. Quality really does trump quantity.

Save money buying these essential garments at budget friendly stores:

Cardigans – Perfect for work, church, and looking chic for grocery store runs. Michelle Obama was the queen of the cardigan, wearing them while campaigning and in the White House as First Lady. She didn't mind sharing that some of her wardrobe was from Gucci, but she also shared her cardigans came from retailers like J Crew, H&M, and White House Black Market. If Michelle Obama can rock a H&M cardigan, then we can learn from her and save money on our cardigans too.

Little Black Dress – It sounds strange that I would place such an imperative dress on my save money list, but I have, and here's why. I have been the belle of the ball many times in a black dress that has come from Goodwill. Many people wear dresses for a formal event one time and take it to Goodwill or a consignment shop. You can find quality black dresses of all different lengths and occasions without anyone knowing that it was a thrift. If thrift stores aren't your thing, then you can also find beautiful black dresses for a reasonable price at department stores, but start at the clearance rack first. Also, look for the dresses before you need it so you don't waste time and money buying in a rush.

Jewelry – Accessories are the best things for a fabulous wardrobe and jewelry is the best accessory to accumulate! The good thing about jewelry is that you can find fabulous jewelry just about anywhere! Pick up jewelry as you travel because it reminds you of places you've visited. I absolutely love the jewelry at Aldo Shoe store and it's trendy, which is why you don't want to spend a lot for it! I've also found great pieces of jewelry from the beauty supply store that totally set off an outfit! Keep your eyes open because fabulous jewelry is all around you, in the least expected places!

T-Shirts/Tank Tops – I love a V-neck T-shirt (you can do so much with them) and I have found that there are many places you can get them in decent quality for a little money. Kohl's and H&M are two stores that I rack up on my T-shirts. I have many white T-shirts because I like them white, and when they don't cost a lot, you can get multiples when they go on sale.

Anything Trendy – Anything that is in style today and out of style tomorrow is not something to invest a lot of money in, so don't spend a lot on trendy pieces. It looks cute for a season and then it sits in the back of your closet or eventually Goodwill will have it. Ask yourself this question when shopping: Will I love this five years from now? If the answer is no, then save your money and put it towards a dream vacation, night out on the town, or an adventure that will have a lasting memory.

CHAPTER 25

PERFUME

No elegance is possible without perfume. It is the unseen, unforgettable, ultimate accessory. – Coco Chanel

I WAS IN MIDDLE SCHOOL when I started wearing perfume. My mother worked at a department store and she would bring samples home that I would try on and instantly I was hooked on smelling good. I learned that getting complimented on how you smell is just as good as getting complimented on how you styled your outfit. Now, I know that no outfit is complete without a pleasant scent! Wearing perfume isn't for special occasions; wearing perfume is part of being a woman of style and class, so it should be worn every day. If you have a favorite scent, that's great, but if you don't, I suggest you make some time to go to a department store and smell different perfumes and try them on until you find a fragrance that you love! When you find a perfume that you love, it will be your signature scent. People will think of you when they smell it, and you'll feel good about not just looking good but smelling good too! Wearing perfume is that little spray of happiness that you can smell throughout the day.

The word *eau* is French for the word *water*. The more water a fragrance has in it the shorter time the scent will last on the body. This is why it is important to know the different kinds of fragrances, what makes some perfumes cost more than others, and what makes some perfume scents last longer.

Here are some definitions to know when fragrance shopping:

Balm Perfume – The balm perfume rolls on so you don't have to spray it. It's great for traveling because it's compact and can be carried in your purse.

Eau De Cologne – The aromatic compound of eau de cologne is 2%–5%, meaning it isn't as concentrated in oil as perfume, but because of this, it makes an expensive bottle of perfume more affordable.

Eau De Toilette – The aromatic compound of eau de toilette is 5%–15%, meaning it's a bit more concentrated in oil than the eau de cologne, but it's not as potent as perfume. This would make it more expensive than the cologne but less expensive than the perfume.

Eau De Perfume – The aromatic compound of eau de perfume is 10%–20%, which means it has more oil than the cologne and toilette. This fragrance can last up to eight hours.

Eau De Parfum – The aromatic compound of eau de parfum is usually 20%–30%, but some go up to 40%. This gives the parfum a higher degree of scent because it has more oil than all of the others. Remember, the higher percentage of oil, the longer the scent will last. This fragrance will be more expensive than all of the other's aforementioned and many are only sold at high-end department stores. The eau de parfum will last all day because it's higher concentrated in oils and fragrance. It should also be noted that quality does not have to be amplified. Less is more when wearing parfum.

Applying perfume:

1. Make sure that the area you're applying your perfume is clean.

2. If the perfume has a lotion in the same scent, then apply the lotion before spraying the perfume so that the perfume lasts longer.

3. Apply perfume on key areas, behind the ears, the neck, behind the knees if you're wearing a dress, and the wrist.

4. Don't rub the perfume in, spray it, and let it settle into your skin.

5. Spray at least 25 centimeters from the skin to avoid spraying too close.

6. Don't overdo it! You want a scent to be pleasant not overwhelming.

7. Learn what scent family you like; is it fresh scents, floral, woody, etc.

A scent is a small detail that makes a big difference. If perfumes are not your thing, then scented lotions have fragrance too. The bottom line is smell good because it compliments looking good!

CHAPTER 26

PICTURE PERFECT

Pictures last a lifetime, so be appropriate and look your best! – Kanika Starr Reynolds

GROWING UP, MY MOM WAS the queen of taking pictures. She captured every moment no matter how beautiful or embarrassing it was. I'm grateful because that gave me a love for taking pictures too. However, there's one big difference between when my mom took pictures and the pictures taken now and it's called social media! With social media being so prevalent, taking pictures of anything, anywhere, with anyone, is the new normal! A bad picture can go viral in a blink of an eye (and so can a fabulous picture) so be mindful of the pictures and poses that you take. When I was a little girl, I would always love looking at the Oscar Awards so I could see the beautiful gowns the actresses would wear. I also loved to see them pose for pictures on the red carpet.

Here are some tips I've picked up along the way to share for your perfect pictures, maybe even for your own red-carpet events! It's like being your very own paparazzi!

1. Keep Makeup to a Minimum. Natural is always better unless you're going to a costume party. Check makeup in good lighting because pictures will catch unmatched foundation on the face that is not on your neck. Make sure highlighter is blended in good because the camera also picks up on highlighter that is too light under the eyes and nose.

2. Shimmer and Glow. Bronzer looks great if applied to the right places. Put a little on your cheekbones and forehead to add warmth and glow. What's left from the brush, shimmer on your neck.

3. Look Smaller. If you're in a picture with other people and you're the curviest ask to be in the middle and sandwich in between them so you look smaller.

4. Look Leaner. Slightly turn your lower body toward the camera and slightly put one leg in front of the other. Stand up straight.

28 Ways to Make it a Choice to Have Great Style

5. Check the little things. Lipstick on teeth, hair out of place, bra straps showing, or oily skin can make a picture that can be extraordinary look mediocre. It's all about the details.

6. Put Down Your Glass. Ditch the wineglass unless you're capturing the toast for a celebration. You may be the life of the party, but the world doesn't need to know that in a picture.

7. Smile Naturally. A fake smile comes across as fake. Show teeth but try not to show too much of your gums. Then think about something or someone that makes you happy. Pleasant thoughts bring about a natural smile.

CHAPTER 27

SELF-LOVE AND SELF-CARE

A woman in harmony with her spirit is like a river flowing. She goes where she will without pretense and arrives at her destination prepared to be herself and only herself. – Maya Angelou

YOU CANNOT OUTRUN YOURSELF. EVERYWHERE you are, you are, and that means that if you're always around yourself, then it's very important to be aware of the things that you're telling yourself. The best way to do this is be intentional about the books you read, television shows you watch, people you're around, and how you use your spare time.

Here are some tips on how to love yourself and care for your well-being so that you can love and care for other's without losing yourself.

28 Ways to Make it a Choice to Have Great Style

1. Connect with God first thing in the morning. The Bible says in Proverbs 20:13 do not love sleep. The first thing that should get our attention should be God not social media. Wake up 15–30 minutes earlier and spend that time with God. I like to read a Proverb a day because the book of Proverbs in the Bible is the book of wisdom. We all need wisdom. There are thirty-one Proverbs in the Bible and there are usually thirty-one days in the month, so whatever day of the month it is, there's a Proverb for that day. I also like to read a Psalm a day because the Psalms are all about praise and praise is always a great way to start the day.

2. Write affirmations about yourself on your bathroom mirror with dry erase markers or on a sticky note and say those affirmations every day out loud before you brush your teeth. I tell myself that I am healthy, wealthy, and wise. Speak it until you believe and become it.

3. Put yourself on the calendar. Do something nice for yourself, things like treating yourself to Starbucks instead of making your own coffee. Go to the movies or watch a movie

on Netflix. Get your hair done, a manicure, pedicure, facial, or a massage. Whatever will make you forget about a stress that you have no control over. Make time for "me" time. Take control over your happiness and mental health.

4. Take a bubble bath.

5. Play your favorite dance song and get up and dance!

6. Research vacations or trips you'd like to take and plan them (even if you don't take them, it's fun to plan.)

7. Watch the sunrise with a cup of coffee or tea.

8. Get quiet and dream! Write down things you'd like to have, do, or be. Use your imagination and dream big!

9. Practice smiling (it keeps wrinkles away too.)

10. Take a walk.

11. Go to the beach or the lake.

12. Try a new cuisine that you've never tried before.

28 Ways to Make it a Choice to Have Great Style

13. Write a list of all of the things you're good at. Call someone close to you and ask them what they think you're good at too. Then do more of these things because using your gift will make you feel good about yourself.

14. Clean out the inside of your car and then wash it at the car wash.

15. Plan to see a local play at the theater.

16. Write a letter to your future self with all of the things you desire to accomplish in a year and then start working on the goals in the letter.

17. Call loved ones and tell them what they mean to you.

18. Buy yourself some flowers. At certain stores behind the floral counter there may be flowers at a reduced rate; check there first.

19. Look at good memories through an old photo album.

20. Pay attention to what you like and don't like. Make learning yourself a priority.

Most woman take care of everyone else, but they forget to take care of themselves. A woman of style knows who she is and that comes by self-discovery and taking the time to learn the essence of what makes them uniquely themselves. There is no one else responsible for your happiness and confidence. That's your job.

I recently read a quote that said, "I was looking for someone to inspire me, motivate me, support me, and keep me focused…. Someone who would love me, cherish me, and make me happy, and I realized that all along I was looking for myself. – Unknown

CHAPTER 28

HAVE FINESSE

Like a gold ring in a pig's snout is a beautiful woman who shows no discretion. – Proverbs 11:22

WE HAVE ALL SEEN BEAUTIFUL women on the outside that open their mouths and say very ugly things that instantly make them unattractive or maybe, you've been that woman. That's why this important final CHAPTER is about finesse. We don't hear this word very often because we live in a world where it seems like everything goes and anything can be said, but there's a time and a place for everything. That is why when a woman has finesse, there is something so beautiful about her. This woman knows how, when, and where to be refined as she handles any situation. I'm sure as you read this book you were able to see that style is not all about fashion and clothes. I've sandwiched fashion and style in between the first CHAPTER of confidence and the last CHAPTER ending with finesse. Without confidence and finesse there is no style. What is finesse? Finesse according to Webster's dictionary is refinement or delicacy. We've covered how to shop, the little black dress, the importance of accessories, and a bevy of other content.

Let's focus on refinement, which is part of having finesse. I can remember having a conversation with my brother one day. As I spoke my mind about some things that I was very passionate about, my voice was loud and I became dogmatic as I tried to drive my point home. I will not forget what he said in his rebuttal to me. He told me, "I lack finesse and I need to work on it." Although my feelings were hurt, I knew he was right. I didn't want to look like I had it all together, but then when I didn't agree with someone, I handled my differences without class. That is why this CHAPTER is so important to me. Women have tried so hard to be heard that we confuse strength with being loud and demanding; it's not. Strength is quiet. It's being slow to speak and quick to listen (James 1:19) so we can respond with finesse. I pray that you are fabulous in every way, not just with fashion and style but with grace, class, and finesse.

APPENDIX A

My Personal Mission Statement _____
_____.

My mission is to improve my self- image by
_____

This will happen when I _____
_____

So that I can_____.

APPENDIX B

My Daily Goals to enhance my self-image

Pray

Meditation

Read Bible/ Devotionals

Exercise

Better Eating Habits

Look Over Written Goals

Visualize My Desired Outcome of the Woman I Desire to Become

Affirmations

APPENDIX C

I Am Affirmations:

I am loved.

I am fabulous.

I am bold.

I am a leader.

I am powerful.

I am joyful.

I am wise.

I am successful.

I am strong.

I am determined.

I am fun.

I am beautiful.

I love myself.

Fill in the blanks and write your own affirmations below

I am _____

I am _____

28 Ways to Make it a Choice to Have Great Style

I am _____

I am _____

I am _____

I am _____

I am _____

I am _____

I am _____

I am _____

Thank you so much for allowing me the pleasure to enhance your beauty with these style tips. Remember that true beauty exudes from within. You feel good about yourself when you work on being the best you that you can be. Do the work to become your best. I pray you never stop striving to be the woman that you imagine yourself to be. I personally love doing the work and with God's grace I will keep evolving. As I grow, I plan to expand and expound on what I've learned. God willing, there will be more books to come.

Much Love,

Kanika Starr Reynolds

About the Author

KANIKA STARR REYNOLDS IS A Michigan native who now resides in Atlanta, Georgia. She is presently fulfilling her purpose of inspiring people globally by way of social media, radio, and television. Kanika is wife to Raymond Reynolds and mother to two teenage daughters and two adult sons. In addition to public speaking, she's also the published author of *Make it a Choice to Have Great Day*.

Raymond and Kanika have been entrepreneurs in Michigan and Georgia for twenty years, owning barber and beauty salons. She is committed to spending her time loving and giving hope to God's people.

Kanika's favorite scripture is "But seek ye first the kingdom of God and His righteousness; and all these things will be added unto you." Matthew 6:33 King James Version

Keep in Touch with the Author:
Facebook : Kanika Starr Reynolds
Instagram: Kanika Starr Reynolds
Email: Kanikastarr1@yahoo.com

Dedication

THIS BOOK IS DEDICATED TO Kyrzada Rodiguez and Dr. MaLinda Sapp. Kyrzada. You were a force in the fashion industry with so much style and grace. Lady MaLinda we both had the same vision to empower and inspire women to love God so that they could in return.

www.ingramcontent.com/pod-product-compliance
Lightning Source LLC
Chambersburg PA
CBHW020426010526
44118CB00010B/444